T0088899

Several other books have been written by me.
If you would like a copy, please do the following:
Send the cost of the book, plus if you live outside of Blairsville, add $3.50 to the cost for shipping.
Each book costs $10.00.

My address is the following:

Dr. Ray Ashurst
P. O. Box 279
Blairsville, GA 30514

The name of the books are as follows:

_____Managing Your Stress
_____Picking Up the Pieces—
Moving On After A
Significant Loss
_____Growing Through Life
_____Healing the Broken Heart
_____Battling Depression—
From Darkness Into Light
_____Friendship—Through Thick and Thin

GOD'S Alive

The Divine Essence of God

James Ray Ashurst, Ph. D.

Cecil Yates, M. S.

BALBOA.PRESS
A DIVISION OF HAY HOUSE

Copyright © 2020 James Ray Ashurst, Ph. D.

All rights reserved. No part of this book may be used or reproduced by any means, graphic, electronic, or mechanical, including photocopying, recording, taping or by any information storage retrieval system without the written permission of the author except in the case of brief quotations embodied in critical articles and reviews.

Balboa Press books may be ordered through booksellers or by contacting:

Balboa Press
A Division of Hay House
1663 Liberty Drive
Bloomington, IN 47403
www.balboapress.com
844-682-1282

Because of the dynamic nature of the Internet, any web addresses or links contained in this book may have changed since publication and may no longer be valid. The views expressed in this work are solely those of the author and do not necessarily reflect the views of the publisher, and the publisher hereby disclaims any responsibility for them.

The author of this book does not dispense medical advice or prescribe the use of any technique as a form of treatment for physical, emotional, or medical problems without the advice of a physician, either directly or indirectly. The intent of the author is only to offer information of a general nature to help you in your quest for emotional and spiritual well-being. In the event you use any of the information in this book for yourself, which is your constitutional right, the author and the publisher assume no responsibility for your actions.

Any people depicted in stock imagery provided by Getty Images are models, and such images are being used for illustrative purposes only. Certain stock imagery © Getty Images.

Scripture quotations taken from the Holy Bible, King James Version (Authorized Version). First published in 1611. Quoted from the KJV Classic Reference Bible, Copyright © 1983 by The Zondervan Corporation.

Print information available on the last page.

ISBN: 978-1-9822-5776-7 (sc)
ISBN: 978-1-9822-5783-5 (e)

Balboa Press rev. date: 10/30/2020

ASSUMPTION

BEFORE YOU BEGIN READING THIS BOOK, THERE IS ONE ASSUMPTION: YOU ARE ASSUMED TO BE ALREADY A BORN-AGAIN CHRISTIAN. IF SUCH IS TRUE, MAY THESE PAGES BE INSPIRING AND ENLIGHTENING.

---jra

ACKNOWLEDGMENTS

My thanks to Cecil Yates,
Michael F. Burrow, and
Col. R. B. Thieme, Jr. who were
instrumental in helping me
produce this book.

Also, to my faithful proofreaders:
Carolyn Baker
Joy Breedlove
Gina Donahue
Carole Peacher

*****

The credit for the beautiful book cover belongs to
Ms. Kelli Denning.

DEDICATION

This book is dedicated to all of those who believe in the power of God and the saving grace of Jesus Christ.

CONTENTS

INTRODUCTION

In the movie, **God's Not Dead**, a young college freshman challenges his atheist professor to prove that God is very much alive and is certainly not deceased. The freshman has to prove to his classmates, his jurists, that God is vibrantly alive. Does he succeed, or does the jury agree with the professor in order to make a decent grade in the class? I challenge you to watch the movie to discover what actually happens.

Christians profess that God is alive, or else they wouldn't be Christians. The basic tenet is that God sent His only Son to earth to pay off our debt of sin so that you and I could have a spiritual relationship with God the Father (John 3:16).

God had to watch his Son be beaten, mocked, and torn to pieces in order to meet the requirement that God demanded. He witnessed the soldiers dragging Jesus to a structure where He was cruelly crucified. There was a point where God had to refuse to come to the rescue of Jesus (Mark 15:34). And for three long days, Jesus was confined to a burial cave. Can you imagine what individuals thought when they saw Jesus walking among them after He left the cave? If it had been me, I would have thought that I was delusional or hallucinating…big time.

Now for the unbelievers, they could simply consider all of this a dramatic story from a make-believe book—the Bible. However, to the believer, the events are as real as real can get. The believer, at some point in his or her life, had to step out in faith and choose to believe that what occurred was actual—very real.

Definition of faith: (1) completetrustorconfidence in someone or something
(2) a strongly held belief or theory

---Google

When I sit down in a chair, I have the faith that its molecules will support my weight. When I get in my automobile, I have the faith that it will start so that I can run my errands. Thus, when I see the wonders of nature, such as the Grand Canyon, I have faith that a living God made them a reality. I know that faith is evidence of an unseen force, and so for me on a personal basis, I have chosen to place my gut feeling of faith in a loving, kind, vibrant, and living Supreme Being. God is not dead and never has been. It is my testimony of faith, and it works for me.

★★★★★ ★★★★★★★★ ★★★★★★★★ ★★★★★★★★

It is at the point where we are
just about to faint, that God
gives us strength to go on.

----anonymous

CHAPTER 1

All-Present

Can any hide himself in secret places that I shall not see him? Do not I fill heaven and earth?
---Jeremiah 23:24

Haven't you wished at times that you could be in two places at the same time? I know that I have. I could get so much more accomplished if it were possible. Well, God can! It truly can boggle one's human mind when trying to comprehend such a concept. Knowing that God is here where I live in Blairsville, Georgia, and in Paris, France, sends chills up me. It does provide comfort and joy to know that wherever I am, God is also there. It is impossible for God to only be in one place at a time. Unlike us, God is not confined to time or space. The complete essence of God is in every place, at the same moment. As humans, we are restricted to a given place at a given time.

You may be sitting on your front porch with the rays of the sun covering you with warmth while at the same exact time, you have a relative who is stationed in Iran, protecting our freedom to sit on our porch. Or, you might have a loved one on a surgery table, about to undergo a minor procedure, and he or she lives hundreds of miles away. God is with you on your porch, in Iran with your family member, and with your friend undergoing surgery. God is in all three places at the exact same time. God cannot and will not abandon the believer no matter where he or she might be. (Hebrews 13:5) The question comes forth, "*If God is in all three locations, why do sad results sometimes happen?*" First of all, God does not cause those results to happen but rather allows them. Secondly, God is not to be held responsible for giving us an explanation of His purpose for allowing things to happen. Thirdly, we are not privy to know the divine plan that God wants to see happen in the lives of His children or in the lives of the involved families. The great comfort is no matter whether we are doing something positive or negative, God says we can't escape his presence. We can't hide from Him. All of us have done some despicable actions in our lives. We now wish we could take them back. We feel ashamed of ourselves, and at times we are haunted by the results of our actions. The guilt can be devastating.

On the other hand, we've done some wonderful, unselfish things for others. We feel good, even proud, of such actions. My dad comes to my mind. He was one of the most giving individuals who inhabited our planet. Yes, he gave his financial resources, but equally given was his time. The giving of one's time, to me, stands out above one's finances because our time is the most important thing we own. My dad was ever-present in lending his time and abilities to friends, family, and strangers. One could always depend on his being present. The same is true of God. His omnipresence is awesome because we are never alone. We may feel it at times, but knowing that we aren't alone is very comforting and important. What a glorious promise He gives us in Hebrews 13:5:

I will never leave thee, nor forsake thee.
--Hebrews 13:5

God occupies both the heavens and our earth at the exact same time. Such a concept can boggle one's mind if we allow it. Our finite mind cannot begin to understand the omnipresence of God—**Psalm 139:6: Such knowledge is too wonderful for me; it is high, I cannot attain unto it.** There are things that we do which make us want to escape God for the time being. No such luck. God's essence can't confine him to one place. Everywhere—God exists. And that is a good thing because we need him to enjoy our successes with us and to hold our hand, so to speak, during our troublesome times.

★★★★★★ ★★★★★★ ★★★★★★ ★★★★★★

God works slowly but surely.
We spoil His work when we
get in a hurry and interfere.
------anonymous

CHAPTER 2

The Mysterious Stranger

In the distance she caught sight of the small church. She felt all alone on this Sunday. The church bells were bonging out as people were entering the country church. Maybe she would find some relief if she joined them. She entered the church but still felt alone even in their midst. Sitting on the very last pew was her custom. Very few, if anyone, sat in such a place. She was trying desperately to focus on the beautiful music coming from the small choir. But her mind kept wandering. She couldn't control her thoughts of despair. She was tempted to quietly make an exit, but the music was compelling—urging her to stay.

She wondered if her family was worried about her whereabouts or if they even cared. Certainly her husband and two sons would manage just fine while she was away for a few hours. She knew that her family loved her, but her loneliness was so very overwhelming. She felt trapped in a continual merry-go-round world. The daily pressures at work and within her home were leaving her desolate and depressed seemingly every minute of her day. Even God seemed to be ignoring her or could care less about her misery. Suicide? Maybe. At least it would be a way out.

The music had stopped, and the pastor asked the congregation to bow their heads in prayer. Just as she lowered her head, someone tapped her on the shoulder.

"Excuse me, young lady," was the whisper. *"May I sit down?"*

"Yes, of course."

When the prayer ended, the two whispered introductions.

"My name is Carl."

"Nice to meet you. I'm Kelli."

The pastor began to make his usual announcements of upcoming events.

"Sorry to come in late."

Kelli smiled. *"No problem."*

"You seemed troubled, Kelli."

"Just life, Carl."

The announcements continued and continued, and the whispering between Kelli and Carl continued. Carl could sense Kelli's sadness. He felt overwhelmed with a burden for her.

The sermon was a 20-minute comfortable, feel-good message. Sitting beside Carl, Kelli felt much at ease. Her feelings of stress and anxiety lightened up, and she was actually in tune to the pastor's delivery of his message. Kelli could feel the tension in her neck and shoulders subside. A warm feeling flowed throughout her body. She realized that she had actually been smiling ever since her conversation had begun with Carl. It had been an awfully long time since she remembered even the slightest hint of a smile.

When the service was over, Kelli and Carl walked out together, exchanging niceties. Kelli happened to remember that she had accidently left her purse inside. She excused herself in order to rescue her handbag. When she returned outside, she couldn't locate Carl in the crowd. He had completely disappeared. Kelli became frantic. She wanted deeply to thank him for his companionship of comfort, kindness, and peace.

Kelli began to ask the remaining church members if they had seen him. She presented a detailed description of Carl. But no one responded. How could anyone disappear so fast? Overhearing Kelli's pleas, an elderly lady timidly approached Kelli.

"Excuse me, young lady. I couldn't help but hear your conversation. I glanced at you several times during the service, and I never saw anyone sitting beside you."

The color drained from Kelli's face.

"But we sat together the whole service! We even talked," exclaimed Kelli.

"I hear what you are saying, but I'm only telling you what I saw and didn't see."

"I'm sorry that I upset you." "Bless you and have a nice day."

★★

Like so many other times and situations, we are left bewildered by supernatural events. Angels unaware make themselves known to us. God is not dead and neither are His messengers.

We are spiritual beings having a physical experience, not physical beings having a spiritual experience.

★★★★★★ ★★★★★★★ ★★★★★★★ ★★★★★★

God requires on our part,
nothing that we are unable,
with His help, to do.
-----anonymous

CHAPTER 3

All-Knowing

God knoweth your hearts.
---Luke 16:15

Another attribute of our living God is his omniscience. He is totally all-knowing. God knows our past, our current situation, and the future challenges that we will be facing. Because He has given us free-will, God does not stop the challenges, whether good or bad, and our responses to them. Yes, we make unhealthy decisions, and they become disastrous. Making such decisions does not mean that God is dead. It means that we made a horrible decision, and the consequences were highly unsuccessful. Did God know that you or I were going to make such a decision? Yes. Why didn't He stop us? Free-will.

Some of the consequences of our decisions catch us totally by surprise. We had expected something else. Do the consequences catch God by surprise? Absolutely not!

Because God knows all things, He knows what is best for us in the long run. When adversities hit us full blast, we have no idea, sometimes, what we are in for. God does. He allows the problems to teach us about some life lessons and of his grace working in our lives.

God knew in eternity past about us even before we were an idea to our parents. God even knew what we would encounter in this life—successes and failures. Whatever we do or don't do, nothing catches God by surprise. He has always known. The fact that you and I were born during this time period rather than 100 years ago or in the future was in God's plan. Our mission is to utilize this time to follow God's leadership and to grow spiritually by leaps and bounds.

God already knows what you are going to do after you finish reading this chapter: my wish is that you use your time wisely and in accordance to what would glorify the omniscient God.

Due to his omniscience, God has always known what each of us would face. In eternity past, God could look down the corridors of time and have complete knowledge of all things. No one can live in this world without experiencing worries and woes. Life is not perfect for anyone. However, no matter how horrible situations can become, God is always present with us. He fully understands our heartache and knows our sadness. He does not cause bad things to happen because we are his children. He allows these things to take place for a divine purpose.

Blaming God for our struggles is a sad waste of time. While in the midst of the problems, we may not see God at work. We may wonder whether we are going to make it through the struggles in one piece. I love the adage that states if we are still alive once the smoke (problems) clears, then God still has a purpose for us.

God's omniscience can provide absolute comfort. He is never shocked about our struggles. He has always been aware of such heartache, and He continues to be by our side through all of it. ***Thank you, Lord.***

★★★★★★★ ★★★★★★★★ ★★★★★★★★★ ★★★★★★★★

God will put the right people
in our life at the right time
and for the right reasons.
-----anonymous

CHAPTER 4

All-Powerful

For with God, nothing shall be impossible.
---Luke 1:37

Some of us grew up watching Superman. He had power and fortitude to capture the villains who were part of the show. We were left mesmerized by his power and how it was used for the common good in society. Superman was our hero because of all the things he could do.

Superman's power is child's play when compared to that of God's. God is omnipotent (all-powerful) which means that no person or vicious animal can force God to yield to any power possessed by a living creature. The atom bomb is like a small firecracker when considering the essence of power in comparing it to God's power.

Because God is all-powerful, He can utilize the dynamics of power that can leave us speechless. We learn of wonderful miracles that take place in the lives of people who are family members and friends. We certainly cannot explain the dynamics involved in the miracle, but we are aware that one has happened. God is in charge of miracles—always has been. Many miracles are recorded in the Bible. The parting of the Red Sea when Moses needed a miracle big time, and Lazarus being brought to life, are two exciting miracles. They are beyond human understanding because they are divinely orchestrated. The desired effect was accomplished according to God's overall plan. Talk about power! As humans, we may well have difficulty trying to understand omnipotence because we are so very limited to space and time.

CHAPTER 5

Goodbye, Dad

The time seemed to drag on and on. The young boy stood by the ornate casket. His dad had suffered horribly with an illness for many months. The boy had watched his robust father waste away, never complaining. He had been a warm, loving father to his only child. The boy was now an orphan, his mom having passed away just a year ago.

While friends approached the casket, they each had something soothing to say to the small boy. But the boy was tuning out all the comments. His attention was on the person lying in the fancy coffin. He tried to stop the sorrowful tears, but the more he tried, the worse they became. Bravely, he fought back the sobs until he was quivering from head to toe. Even the soft expressions from those in attendance bounced off little Tony. He felt so alone and scared. His mind began to be scattered with all kinds of haunting thoughts. As much as he tried, he couldn't stop them.

"What's going to happen to me?"
"Who am I going to live with?"
"Who's going to take me on father-son activities?"

"If God is love like everyone has always told me, why did he let my dad die?"
"Life is not fair and never will be."

Tony had been told many times by his father to be real strong and brave when he was no longer around. Out of respect, he promised his dad that he would try. But that was a lie. He was falling apart. He was angry with God and wanted nothing to do with Him.

Tony couldn't get out of his mind how mean God was to take his dad away. "Why would God do that?" wondered the son. His little heart was breaking apart. The tears continued as people kept filing past the casket.

Tony thought of all the places his dad wouldn't be around to take him to, such as football practices, school plays, piano lessons, his high school graduation, even his marriage if he decided to get married. Tony felt distraught and very lonely. "What will I do?"

Tony felt a hand on his shoulder. He looked up to see an older gentleman looking down at him. The old man had a gentle smile which went well with his face.

"Tony, I know you are hurting real bad, and I'm sorry."

"It just isn't fair," whispered Tony in response.

"To you, son, it isn't. I wish I could change it for you."

"Why is God so mean that he killed my dad?"

"Well, it wasn't God. It was your dad's illness."

The old gentleman took a deep breath.

"Tony, the Bible tells us that God loves you and yes, your dad too. God loves us when bad things happen to good people. God continues to love us."

Tony wiped away his tears on his coat sleeve. *"I just don't get it."*

"Of course you don't, and neither do I. Understanding why God allows some things to happen can be confusing to us.You just have to trust that He is doing things for a reason. Can you try doing that?"

"I suppose, but I'm still sad.

"It's okay to be sad. You're supposed to be. You loved your dad a whole lot."

Tony looked at his father in the casket.

"He's gone forever."

"No, son. He hasn't left you. You see, he's just changed his address."

Tony smiled.

CHAPTER 6

Truth

For his merciful kindness is great toward us; and the truth of the Lord endureth forever. ----Psalms 117:2

God is ultimate truth. He is not capable of being deceitful and untruthful, nor misguiding to us. Since He deals with everyone in truth, we know that He loves and cares for each of us because we are told such throughout the Scriptures. Because God deals solely in the truth, all of his promises are ours to hold dear.

Morning, noon, and night I complain and groan, and he listens to my voice. Psalms 55:17

The Lord is compassionate, merciful, patient, and always ready to forgive. Psalms 103:8

I am convinced that nothing can ever separate us from God's love which Christ Jesus our Lord shows us. ---Romans 8:38

But the Lord is faithful and will strengthen you and protect you against the evil one. ---II Thess. 3:3

God didn't give us a cowardly spirit but a spirit of power, love, and good judgment. II Tim. 1:7

God loved the world this way: He gave his only Son so that everyone who believes in Him will not die (spiritually) ***but will have eternal life. ---John 3:16***

But nothing is impossible for God. ---Luke 1:37

God's choice does not depend on a person's desire or effort, but on God's mercy. ---Romans 9:16

All of the promises in God's Word demonstrate his love for us. God is faithful to back up the promises as well as to love us without any strings attached. Unlike so many humans, God's love has no conditions. It takes a lot of concentration to wrap our minds around such love. If we are to know who and what God is, then we can find out by delving into His Word. I love the Scripture that claims: **In the beginning was the Word, and the Word was with God, and the Word was God** (John 1:1). God has always dealt with mankind in truth. God and Truth are the same. God is the absolute truth—Deut. 32:4b. That gives us comfort and assurance.

God's faithfulness is backed by his veracity. His truth guarantees that He will do what He says and nothing happens by chance or luck. Since God cannot lie, whatever He has claimed will be so. When our life seems as if it is going to fall apart, it isn't. God's truth is that He has you and me in his care. God loves His children just as human parents do. God may well allow hardships to invade one's arena, but they don't diminish His infinite love. We can learn many life lessons from such troubles and emerge intact. We will have a sense of stability by claiming God's truths—His promises.

God's truth also contains His warnings. God knows what we need to do to have an abundant life and yet He also knows what will interfere with our fellowship with Him.

There are three ways in which our fellowship with God is disrupted. One way is when we take our focus and our attention off of God and place it on ourselves.

For the children of Israel have forsaken the covenant—I Kings 19:10a

By focusing on ourselves, we at times have the experience of self-pity. We feel sorry for ourselves and forget that God will take care of our burdens when we let go of them. We tend to panic rather than trust God to handle whatever is bothering us. Can you recall a big worry that you had last month or a year ago? Well, you are still here, aren't you? Whether it turned out the way you wanted or not, you are still alive and a-kicking. When we focus on ourselves, we are usually dealing with our personal desires and ego-wants. Our attention is on self rather than staying true to God's Word.

Another way we get out of fellowship with God is placing our focus on people.

Thus saith the Lord. cursed be the man that trusteth in man—Jer. 17:5a.

When God takes second place to family, including our own children, or our close friends, we are heading for real trouble. God wants always to be first in our life, in our decisions. God is not to be seen as a "convenient God" –that is, we give Him our attention when it's convenient. He doesn't work that way. He is **#1** or not at all. And the decision is ours.

A third way in which we have fellowship problems with God is when we put our attention on things.

Let your manner of life be without covetousness and be content with such things as ye have—Hebrews 13:5

Finances are a biggie. We just don't seem or think that we have enough, so we "sell our souls" to get more, more, and more. Of course we might give a pittance to the church or to a charity, so that we can feel good. However, we "live and breathe" to get more, thus neglecting God in the meantime. We are putting up a barrier between God and us. It is definitely **not** wrong "to make" money, but not at the expense of our righteous fellowship with the Father.

We at times lose sight of God because we are so occupied with our orientation to success in the public and private sense. We should strive to be successful at work and with our family. Nothing wrong with that. However, spending 92 percent of one's time reaching for success can be a disaster. We are probably neglecting God, our family, and our friends. What a terrible shame! One's occupation is vitally important, but not at the cost of sacrificing those who love us.

Redeeming oneself to God is needed if we have ignored Him. His love is continual and will always be ours.

CHAPTER 7

Sovereignty

God who made the world and all things in it, seeing that he is Lord of heaven and earth—Acts 17:24

God is the ultimate Supreme Being of the universe which includes heaven and earth. It is quite impossible for us to wrap our finite minds around an always-existing God. We try to make sense of it, but our three pounds of brain matter just cannot do it. Never have, never will. God has been eternal—never a beginning, never an end. It might serve us well to stop trying to make sense of it all, and simply by faith, believe the Scriptures.

Because God is Sovereign, He doesn't have to seek out permission to determine what is to transpire in His universe. God has a marvelous divine plan for each believer's life and has the ultimate authority and power to bring it to happen. He promotes the believer towards success in His own timing. We don't reach our peak due to luck or by our own merits. God oversees our goings and comings in life, and because of His grace, we are blessed.

God's discernment has assigned **all** things their respective places. God has use of all things in His creation, or else they wouldn't exist. Whether creatures or plants, God has assigned them a proper function.

Because He is the Creator, God possesses all things. He owns them all. What we have belongs to Him, and God is simply loaning them to us for the time being—**For every beast of the forest is mine, and the cattle upon a thousand hills—Psalms 50:10**. God is permitting us to temporarily possess certain material things. From the smallest to the largest of possessions, each belongs to the Creator.

We belong to God means He has authority over us. We've been purchased with an extravagant price (the blood of Jesus Christ). We may not align ourselves up with God at times—we are given free will. However, God's sovereign nature continues to have authority and possession over us.

It offers great comfort and assurance to us knowing that God's sovereignty is in control of the world in which we live. Nothing evil can destroy or annihilate our world because it all belongs to God. It is loaned to us to enjoy and to preserve.

CHAPTER 8

Justice

**Let the fear of the Lord be upon you: take heed and do it; for there is no iniquity with the Lord our God, nor respect of persons—
II Chronicles 19:7**

When an individual is in court, having to face a judge about his or her wrongdoing, the person hopes that the judge is fair and quite trustworthy.

God represents justice in its purest sense. When God has to make a judgment call, one can count on it being totally fair. When the world, as we know it, comes to an end, God's justice will prevail. His justice is intact now, in the past, and throughout eternity. Whatever God plans to do at the end of time will be out of His justice. God will deal with believers, unbelievers, demons, and Satan.

God's plan for us is magnificent, and His justice ensures that His plan will be acted upon. If the individual is determined, by his free will, to stay in God's will, then God's justice (fairness) will be in operation.

There are times when we hear or even see individuals transact unjust things. We sense that they even know the wrong that they are committing, and what makes things worse, they seem to be getting away with it. In our mind we wonder where God is in all of this? If He is pure justice, why doesn't He put a stop to it right then and there.

Where is God?

His fairness seems to be lacking, and we become angry and confused. God is the one who claimed that vengeance was His (Deuteronomy 32:35a), so where is it?

We want God to act swiftly regarding the wrongdoing, as if we are purely clean.

CHAPTER 9

Grace

The Lord will give grace and glory. No good thing will He withhold from them that walk uprightly—Psalms 84:11

Just as we cannot fathom the divine love of God, neither can we come close to understanding and to appreciating the dynamics of God's unmeasurable grace. It is His grace that allows us to be a part of His royal family. His grace stems from a pure kindness and love from our heavenly Father.

From His perfect goodness, God showers grace on us even though we are totally unfit in nature. We certainly have not earned nor deserved His grace, but God gives it to us on a daily basis. Not a single day goes by that we aren't the fortunate recipients of experiencing grace to the maximum. The mere fact of waking up each morning is a grace gift. Having been able to pay your monthly bills (or most of them) is a demonstration of his grace. Everything that is of God or from Him is a manifestation of His pure majesty. His grace never dies. It keeps giving and giving. God's love for us bestows grace in our lives in order for us to be humble and to be obedient to Him. All of us have probably heard of individuals who brag about being self-made. No such person has ever existed! For the successful believer, and even the unbeliever, it has always been the grace of God in front of and behind the individual.

Divine grace is absolutely indispensable because it is based on who and what God is, and not on our personal merits. We don't have the right or merit to receive God's grace. He has chosen to give it freely to the individual even though the person may not have the foggiest idea concerning the elements of grace.

Mankind benefits from God's grace: our salvation, everlasting life, love from God and all personal material possessions originate from the awesome grace of God. As unworthy creatures, grace allows us to have a relationship with a holy God. We can have a wonderful, righteous relationship with Him because of His loving grace.

Grace is always triumphant because it is based on the sovereignty of God. Even Satan's evil cannot destroy the power of God's grace for the believer. He can try using his evil tactics against the believer, but he is no match against God's omnipotence. God's grace is a continuing success in spite of Satan's evil behavior.

God provides for the believer numerous grace opportunities.

We are ambassadors for Christ,
as though God did beseech you by us.
We beg you in Christ's stead,
Be ye reconciled to God.
II Corinthians 5:20

As ambassadors we have the opportunity to portray Christ through our behavior and speech. People are curious creatures, much like cats. When unbelieving persons see and hear our Christian witness, they may well wish to know more. It is a wonderful opportunity to demonstrate what the grace of God is all about.

God empowers our spiritual life because of His grace in our lives—Ephesians 3:16-19. There is no limit to what a person can accomplish in his or her spiritual life when in tune with the grace and love of God.

Because God is eternal and cannot die or dissipate into nothing, His grace is the same. His grace can never die. It keeps giving and giving. Grace's impact on our behalf is greater than we can ever imagine. What God gives us from His grace is backed by an all-powerful God. Also, His grace is backed by the greatest power in the universe.

This can be mind-boggling when we attempt to wrap our finite minds around it. So, my suggestion is to save yourself the trouble, relax, and accept it in accordance with the Scriptures.

The power of grace reigns supreme and is continually in production within each believer. Grace is even evident within the believer who has turned his or her back on the living God. The power of grace is awesome—Romans 5:20-21. Grace guarantees that we will have eternal life with God because His grace has won over our old nature and reigns supreme within us. Talk about power! God's grace is magnificent (which is indeed an understatement).

We cannot in our own power earn the grace of God. It is freely given as a divine gift at the point of salvation. This gift is our means of appreciating God for all the things He does for us for the remainder of our lives throughout eternity. What a gift!

When understanding the grace of God, one must look at the entire essence of God. Each essence demonstrates the wonderful grace that God gives to us. He is grace, and we are the recipients.

The results of grace can be seen in every wonderful thing we have or will have. Grace belongs to God, and He freely gives it to us as His children. Look around you: your home, your property, your garden, your clothes, your family, and so much more are the vivid result of God's living grace in our lives. We are truly blessed now and forever. Because of who and what God is, we receive the marvelous benefits of grace.

God's love for us has always been in operation as a result of His grace. From the day we were conceived, God bestowed His perfect love and grace in our lives. We can always count on God to treat us in love and with grace. On the days when we are mean, irritable, and plain nasty, we still will be treated in grace. God has to because that's part of His essence. God's grace is not unstable—it is constant and reliable because that is who God is—all the time. We certainly don't deserve it, but it is ours to claim in His name. If His grace depended on who and what we are, we would get absolutely nothing, and we would be in big trouble.

We don't deserve or earn the right to be successful in our profession. It is due to God's grace. The grace of God paves our way to success and to abundant living. His grace is for every believer, for even individuals who have rejected Him. Grace is the work of God on our behalf. Grace is all that the Mighty God is free to do for mankind. God is constantly waiting to pour out His grace on every single believer, for even those who have rejected Him. **And therefore will the Lord wait, that he may be gracious unto you and therefore will He be exalted—Isaiah 30:18.**

★★★★★★★ ★★★★★★★ ★★★★★★★★ ★★★★★★★

Life is good because
God is great.
----anonymous

CHAPTER 10

Never Changing

The everlasting God, the Lord, the Creator of the ends of the earth, fainteth not, neither is weary. There is no searching of His understanding—Isaiah 40:28

One of my favorite verses in the Scriptures is Hebrews 13:8—**Jesus Christ, the same yesterday, and today, and forever**. To know that God has always been the same is comforting and reassuring. Unlike us human beings who are constantly changing, God is the same God one hundred years ago that He is today in this 21st century. God cannot change—Psalms 102:12—**But thou, O Lord, shalt endure forever, and thy remembrance unto all generations.** Long before mankind came into being, God was in existence and even then was the same as He is today. Do you want to know what God was before us? Simply read the Scriptures. What the authors of the Bible proclaimed about God was true before the Bible was written. Nothing has changed about God. If we no longer feel close to God, guess who has moved? It isn't God. He can't change course. God is "eternal"—no beginning and no end. Whereas man is "everlasting"—a beginning and no end. God's immutability cannot be tarnished, destroyed, or changed. This is what gives us confidence in His Word and in His ultimate Plan for our individual lives. This should place a big smile on each of our faces.

Just think: Because God is immutable, His love for us can never change. Even when we are at our very worst, God still gives us divine love. What a glorious God! When our mean streak is in control, God's grace, plus His love and forgiveness, is ever-present. Such is the magnificence of God. His ultimate love is always! Enduring love is based on who and what God is, **not** on our character. It's mind-blowing for me to even conceive of such perfect love and grace. It never can change because God can't.

The beauty of God's immutability is that He offers absolute stability. We do not have a wishy-washy God. His essence is stable—the God we worship today will be the same God we worship 20 years from this date. That's stability! Do you think we will be same one year from now, much less 20 years in the future? I think not. God will. His stability guarantees it. We indeed are very blessed individuals.

Since God cannot change, neither can his Word—I Peter 1:25—**But the word of the Lord endureth forever**. All that God has declared in Scripture is just as valid today as it was when the first word was written. By faith we believe, and thus it becomes real to us. All the promises that God has given us are alive today. Hundreds of promises belong to us—all we have to do is claim them as ours. They belong to us. The unchanging God gave them to us as His divine gifts. And God's stability backs up each one of them.

CHAPTER 11

Love

He that loveth not knoweth not God for God is love—I John 4:8

Trying to wrap our finite minds around the love of God is perhaps difficult.. His love comprises everything we know about love and much more. Our capacity to understand divine love from a human viewpoint is quite impossible.

God is perfect in His unchanging love. He can't stop loving us and wanting the best for us even if we don't deserve it. He never stops His divine love, and it has endured from the very day we were born to our current age into the future.

When we were disciplined by our parents for misbehaving, we found it impossible to believe that it was from their source of love. At the time, love was the very last motive in their hearts in our youthful mind. God is no different. When we are experiencing divine discipline, it has God's love behind it. God does not punish His children for the fun of it. He does it to help get us straightened out so that we can be in His will once again. Such is the love of the Almighty God.

We can speak of God's love with great gratitude. We just never will fully understand the dynamics on this side of heaven. It is God's grace that bestows such love upon us. We don't deserve His grace nor earn it, but God gives it freely to us. The same can be true of our own parents. They have a love that never quits, and it lasts forever and a day. No matter how we disappoint them, nothing really separates their wonderful love from us. Their love is based purely on who and what they are, not on who and what we are. Such love is similar to divine love. No matter how rotten we behave, God's love never changes.

God loves the unbeliever just as much as the believer. The reason being that His love operates always and totally at a maximum level. The unbeliever has every chance to return a love for God. In turn, the believer returns love for God by knowing Him better through studying His Word—getting to know exactly who God is.

The more we know about God, the more we can appreciate His grace and phenomenal love. Since God knew us in eternity past (omniscience), His love for us has always been perfect. What a great awareness that is for us.

Even though we are spiritual beings having a human experience, we still have no concept of the depths of divine love. It goes deeper than the deepest ocean and beyond the sky that we see each day. No matter who you are or what you have done, you can count on the love of God. His love is based on His essence which is perfect, great, and stable.

The greatest demonstration of love is Jesus Christ paying for the sins of humanity whether people confess or disavow Him.

****** ******* ******** ********

God loves us in a moment
than anyone could in a lifetime.
-----anonymous

CHAPTER 12

Eternal Life

For thus saith the Lord who created the heavens, God himself who formed the earth and made it—Isaiah 45:18

There are things that we humans will never ever totally comprehend, such as the intricacies of pregnancy. Another mind-boggler, an amazing fact, is the eternal life of God. Where did He originate? How long has He been in existence? Who really is He, and will He cease to exist one day? Questions after more questions. As curious beings, we desire honest answers. And yet we remain perplexed…and ultimately frustrated because we have no answers to some of our questions. We read theological books with the high hopes that answers are within. But those writers have no concrete answers either. So the search continues.

From me to you: your search is futile.

God helps us with some of our searching questions: He has **always** existed! **And God said unto Moses, I Am That I Am—**Exodus 3:14. God is in the present tense: **I keep being who I am being.** God never speaks of Himself in a past tense because He can't. God's existence is so concrete, so very perfectly absolute. From eternity past to **always** into the future, God will "be" –never a time when "been" is a characteristic describing God.

No matter what type of troubles we encounter in our earthly life, God has always been our "shelter" from the day of our birth into our everlasting life with Him. That's not to say that we aren't going to have challenging problems confront us. For whatever reasons, God allows confrontations to visit our arena. Some are quite nasty. We may never know the reason "why" but God knows.

Every single situation, whether good or bad, that comes our way is absolutely no surprise or shock to Him. After all, He is eternal—He was there when the problems came our way, plus He knew about them (omniscience). The situations can well catch us unaware, but not God.

As you think about God, is it difficult to imagine that He is absolute—no beginning and no ending? If it is hard to wrap your mind around such a marvelous concept as God's eternal life, then join the club. It is way beyond our creative imagination. Because God has no beginning or end, time is non-essential, unlike the deadlines facing us human beings.

Our watches/clocks dictate our day's agenda, but not so with God. Try an experiment: when you get up one morning, go for eight hours without looking at a timepiece—no cheating! Welcome to God's world.

Before God created the world in which we live, what did God do in eternity past? Curious? Me too. I don't believe for one second that God "sat" idly by, bored to tears. To find out what He did will require patience—meaning to wait to ask Him when we see him face-to-face.

God is in control of our world. He is alive and will forever be the master of it, long after we have ascended.

CHAPTER 13

Righteousness

There is none holy like the Lord—I Samuel 2:2

Sometimes it is difficult to admit that we have done many things wrong during our brief time on earth. Our unrighteousness is clouded over by all the good things that we have done. However, we are a far cry from being the perfect person we may try to be. Most individuals who are part of our arena never witness our "bad side" –only our "good side" on any given day.

God's absolute righteousness or His holiness is incomparable. There is no creature that can be compared to the holiness of God. He is absolute!

God knows no sin because He is perfect—**God is light and in him is no darkness at all—I John 1:5.** The perfect character of God gives us comfort in knowing that the God we worship has never committed any sin. Unlike us, God's righteousness is like a brilliant light. There is no way that we can ever measure up to a perfect God, but yet His grace and forgiveness allow us to have a magnificent relationship with Him. Such is the glory of God.

God's forgiveness is similar to our earthly parents'. All of us have done things that didn't meet the approval of our mom and dad. We got caught misbehaving. I remember as a young lad stealing some chocolate candy from a nearby grocery store. My mother caught me stuffing all the candy in my mouth at once. Instead of owning up to it, I said my best friend, Gail, gave me the pieces. Oh Oh! Stealing and lying. But my mother forgave me once the truth came out. (I had to tell the owner of the grocery store what I had done. Talk about embarrassment.) I didn't earn or deserve my mother's forgiveness (or the store owner's), but I received it.

God's righteousness is perfect and yet He forgives our mistakes—our errors—our unrighteous behavior. Our minds may be boggled when trying to comprehend God's perfect attitude and actions. Rather than trying to wrap our minds around such a marvelous attribute of God, it is best to give our brains a break and accept it by our trust in Him.

God treats us in grace which is based on His love and righteousness. Since both are perfect, His grace towards us is perfect. We all will go through hardships, but He has it all under control. There is never a time when He is surprised and out of control. We may think He is, but the perfect God knows and understands. We are the ones who are probably out of control, but…never the Almighty God.

Worshipping a perfect God gives us the assurance that He hears our requests and absolutely answers each one. Some answers are "yes" while others are "no" and the others are "wait" for now. He does **not** answer with a "maybe" because God's omniscience knows what is best for us at the time, according to His plan for our lives. The perfection of God guarantees it.

CHAPTER 14

Sense of Humor

Have you ever wondered if God has a sense of humor? It might be difficult for us to conceive of the Almighty God having a humorous sense comprising His character. Many of us have probably never heard a sermon regarding God having a sense of humor. I'm not talking about an out-of-control, laughing, hysterical God. However, Biblical situations did occur that are humorous from a human and divine viewpoint.

When the prodigal son got too big for His britches and decided that at an early age he could make it on his own, to be self-sustaining, he left home. Of course God knew that the prodigal son was nowhere ready to go out on his own. However, God paved the way for "the boy" to venture out and explore the world.

There is no doubt that God did not find it humorous regarding the conflicts that the young son encountered when away from home. God does not take any joy in the problems that we get into when we are out of His plan for us. It breaks "God's heart" to see us in negative ordeals. God allows them but does not cause the situations.

Can you imagine what the son was going through as he returned home? Would his father accept or reject him? Would the father lay a guilt trip on him? The father certainly had the right to do so. However, that didn't happen. His father was overjoyed to have his son home safe, sound, and sane.

There is a divine parallel in the story. When we get out of His plan for us, we resemble the young son. We get ourselves into all sorts of trouble. However, when we do return to God's will, we are welcomed back. Like the father of the prodigal son, ultimate love and grace and forgiveness remain intact. They never diminish or change. God treats us the very same.

Another humorous side of God is found in the life of David. God is in charge of promoting us in life. We don't have the power to do it on our own. It is the grace of God that takes us where we are to where He wants us to be.

One has to appreciate the humor of God in the exciting story of David. As a young boy, David had no earthly idea that God was going to promote him to be a "great among the great" –David was clueless, but God wasn't. God knew that David was going to rise to the ultimate, and David's faithfulness, devotion, and love for God were reasons for his promotion to become the greatest king in the Old Testament.

God's sense of humor is most often detected when He has situations in which He demonstrates His mighty power over individuals. This is the story of Onesimus, a house-slave of Philemon. The humor of God in this story is similar to that of the Prodigal Son. Each thought he could make it in the world on his own and without God. In his humor, God allowed each to find out, on his own, how much each needed the Lord in his or her life and what the power of grace can do for a person.

In the city of Colosse, there was a house-slave named Onesimus. He belonged to a Christian named Philemon, a pastor of a local church in that city. Onesimus stole some of his master's money and fled to Rome. He apparently led a riotous life in Rome, using up his master's money. He soon ran out of funds and began to be in desperate need of help.

In Rome, Onesimus remembered his master had often spoken of someone who was in Rome in prison (house arrest), the Apostle Paul. In Rome, Onesimus searched for Paul and found him. The contact of the thief, Onesimus, with the Apostle Paul resulted in Onesimus believing in Jesus Christ as Lord and Savior. As a result of his regeneration, he studied under Paul, learned doctrine, and grew in grace toward spiritual maturity.

Onesimus became a great help to Paul. Paul, in his letter to Philemon, is about to send him back to Colosse and to the house of Philemon. One day in the future, Philemon would open the door, and there would stand the run-away slave, Onesimus. He would be different now. He left a run-away slave and thief and returned as a born-again believer.

Once in the house of Philemon, Onesimus handed Paul's letter to his master. This letter is now a part of God's word, the Book of Philemon. The letter is short and personal. This story is about three great believers who, through spiritual maturity, were helpful to each other.

Another story that demonstrates God's sense of humor is found in Isaiah 36-37. The time period was around 710 BC. Israel was being assaulted by the Assyrians via King Sennacherib and his large and powerful army under the command of a man named Rabshakeh. Rabshakeh appeared at Jerusalem demanding that Israeli King Hezekiah surrender to the Assyrian forces.

Just prior to this, the remaining spiritual remnant of Israel fled from Jerusalem—Isaiah 37:31-32, to the little town of Libna, one of the 76 cities surrounded with walls. In leaving Jerusalem, they took their books, scripts, and other spiritual materials with them to Libna. The heart of the spiritual life of Israel was then being housed in little Libna.

Considering the difficulty of scaling the walls of Jerusalem, the Assyrian army moved to destroy the town of Libna under the command of the Assyrian king, Sennacherib. He collected an army of 185,000 soldiers, surrounded the town, and built great siege works around it in preparation of an assault the following day. During the night, the Angel of the Lord "went forth and smote in the camp of the Assyrians a hundred and fourscore and five thousands," –Isaiah 37:36. In the morning, "behold they were all dead corpses." Only the king survived. He returned to Nineveh. Soon after, while he was worshiping his god Nisroch, his two sons "smote him with the sword," –Isaiah 37:38.

The spiritual ignorance of the Assyrian King and his vile attitude toward Israel and God sealed his end. The Assyrians put their trust in themselves and their powerful army up against the Lord God of Israel. Something they failed to recognize in their ignorance was the Jewish remnant inside the walls of helpless little Libna.

The humor in this story is evident. God allowed the Assyrians to continue to blaspheme Him, rely on their own self-confidence, their own power, equipment, and army. Libna was severely limited in power, weapons, and soldiers. The thing in their favor was the Lord in their hearts. In this battle, no shots were fired, no arrows shot, and no stones thrown. Yet, they were delivered. Ecclesiastes nine tells of the wisdom (doctrine) in one poor man's soul that was the true weapon of deliverance—**But there was found in it a poor (mistreated) man (full) of doctrine, and he delivered the city by means of his doctrine (in his soul). But no one remembered that poor man (remains unknown to human history).**

The humor of God is evident when one reads the Red Sea Adventure (Exodus 14:21-31;15:12). The mighty Pharaoh thought honestly that he had the power to destroy one of the greatest believers in the Bible—Moses. God must have gotten a "humorous kick" out of watching the

Pharaoh chasing Moses, believing he was finally going to destroy Moses and the people of Israel.

Having survived the plagues of Egypt, the Pharaoh and his army did not give up in attempting to destroy Moses and the people of Israel. As the Jews began their journey home, the Egyptians were gripped with rage. They failed to see that their battle was with the God of Israel rather than the Jewish people. Filled with anger against them, Pharaoh and his army began to pursue. This effort led them up to the Red Sea. The hand of God preserved the Jews with a cloud by day and a pillar of fire by night. However, this did not deter the efforts of the Egyptians.

God then opened up a path through the Sea via His breath, holding up the waters on either side. He dried up the floor of the sea so Israel could walk across the Sea on hard dry land. The Egyptians pursued. Then God caused the Egyptians to be covered with the water, destroying Pharaoh and his entire army. The Egyptians failed to realize whom they were up against. But God knew.

DAVID AT VALLEY OF ELAH
I Samuel 17

Israel was at war with the Philistines. Each army had an estimated 50,000 soldiers. They had confronted each other in the Valley of Elah (30 miles southwest of Jerusalem). The army of Israel held the hill to the north of the valley, while the Philistines were on the south. A nine-foot tall giant of a man named Goliath was the

Philistine champion who came forth each day for forty days and issued a challenge to Israel for them to put forth their champion for an individual battle. Whoever won, the other side would totally surrender its armed forces.

David, relieved from watching over his father's sheep, was sent to take food and other things to three of his brothers, plus some special items to King Saul. As he showed up at Elah, the giant came forward and issued the challenge again, saying, "I defy the armies of Israel this day."

David asked, "Who is the Philistine, that he should defy the armies of the living God?" Young David was the only one who had divine clarity of mind as to who was going to win the battle. He would reveal the power of God to his own people. For this, David was mocked by his brothers and others at the moment. But, David was persistent. He stated, "…the Lord will deliver me out of the hand of this Philistine." He was presented to King Saul who doubted the outcome for Israel, but allowed David to meet the giant in battle.

David collected five smooth stones from the brook for use with his sling. David would only need one stone.) Goliath had four giant sons behind him. David was relying upon the Lord for deliverance. The giant's gods were his spear, sword, shield, helmet, and coverings of brass. The giant's faith was in these gods. The giant disdained David and cursed David. David told the giant that the Lord would deliver him into His hand and that the assembly would know that the Lord "saveth not with sword and spear for the battle is the Lord's" and that he would give the giant into "our hands." (Israel) One small stone won the battle. The Philistines were defeated.

One can begin seeing God's humor at this point. Goliath thought that he had the power and strength to outdo the Almighty God. Even more humorous was that God used a young boy to put Goliath, the powerful Philistine, in his place—on the ground, dead. One can only sense the imaginary conversation among God, David, Goliath, and David's brothers.

God to Goliath: *Okay, big boy. Let's see how you make out this time with a young kid who has never been to the military academy."*

God to David's brothers: *"Ok, boys, you can stop having a panic attack. Stand by and watch what a real soldier and hero your little brother is."*

God to David: *"How did you like that small smooth stone I made for you? I made that stone for you a long time ago. I and that little stone have been waiting on you for over a thousand years."*

****** ******* ******* *******

God has a bigger plan for us
than we have for ourselves.

-----anonymous

CHAPTER 15

Faithfulness

Creation was not an accident. God created the heaven and the earth. He did so in a specific way for a specific purpose, Genesis 1, 2. Time, as we presently experience it, consists of His moving all things toward the completion and fulfillment of His goals and purpose. His plan is to ultimately bring the heaven and the earth into perfect unity with each other as He had planned since creation. Through His faithfulness toward us, the result will be a glorious everlasting existence that He will share with us as believers.

All things were created by Him. Everything in heaven and on earth, visible and invisible, was made for Him and exists for His present use and ultimate divine purpose, Col 1:16-17. "All things" are involved in His moving forward to conclude His final glorious purpose. God has **predetermined** that nothing in Heaven nor on Earth can stop this movement. "Everything" is in motion toward this divine fulfillment under His **righteous** direction. His righteousness guarantees that His faithfulness cannot fail, and it also insures our eternal future with Him.

Historically, Satan has gone to great lengths to interrupt this movement. His interruptions began in

Heaven (Isaiah 14:12-15) and then on Earth (Genesis 3:1-6). Satan continues to utilize his own strategy of evil in pursuing the frustration of God's plan and purpose at all costs. Satan cannot win. God's strategy will succeed through His faithfulness toward His ultimate objective.

We become "an epistle of Christ," II Corinthians 3:2-3, reflecting to the world the light and life of God, His thinking, His character, His righteousness, and his faithfulness. What a privilege it is to share this information with others.

Out of his omniscience comes the thinking process of "**forethought**" or "**foreknowledge.**" God possesses the capacity to see into the future concerning individuals, events, and circumstances. He knows what is going to happen regarding each of us, and the faithfully attempts to prepare us to deal in a godly manner with future problems and with those things we are unable to see or predict—Proverbs 3:13-18. This matter of His forethought is a very precious gift for each of us.

We see the characteristics of divine forethought and faithfulness at work in many instances in the Bible, such as David slaying Goliath, the giant, and the crossing of the Red Sea. In the Old Testament these events were physical. These events illustrated to the existing world the power of God in the lives of individuals and nations. In our present age, these characteristics are at work within us.

In spite of setbacks to Satan's strategies, he also attempts to separate each of us from God's love. Satan has a set of tactics he uses against each of us as believers (Romans 8:35-36). These tactics include ***"...tribulation or distress, or persecution, or famine, or nakedness, or peril, or sword."*** Most of us encounter on a regular basis the first of these tactics: **tribulation.** This consists of our regular "troubles" of life, large and small. God allows these to occur to us as tests of life and of dependency on Him. In His continuing faithfulness toward each of us, He has provided within us the traits to make each of us **"overcomers,"** (Romans 8:37-39. In His **forethought**, He saw each of our problems. God is absolutely faithful on a very personal basis. **"It is of the Lord's mercies that we are not consumed, because His compassions fail not. They are new every morning: great is thy faithfulness,"** Lamentations 3:22-23.

In the passages of scripture, we find the term "righteousness of God" being used in conjunction with the term "faithfulness of God." These terms belong together. His faithfulness always is of a divine nature with a divine objective in mind. His righteousness insures His integrity in all that He decides and does.

God is happy to share the two characteristics of faithfulness and righteousness with those who trust in Him. David acknowledged this in I Samuel 26:23: **The Lord render to everyman His righteousness and His faithfulness..."** Each believer actually shares in the life of God. The moment one believes in Christ as Saviour, the righteousness of God is faithfully given to that person forever. When God looks at each of us, He sees His own righteousness within.

All the characteristics of God were magnificently displayed in the historic event of David, the shepherd boy, slaying the giant Goliath (I Samuel 17). It was God's foreknowledge and faithfulness that brought together the perfect timing, environment, and circumstances to demonstrate how His faithfulness brings His grace and power to bear through simple people who trust and put their faith in Him.

In the Valley of Elah, where the battle between Goliath and David occurred, God placed the brook with running water in order to smooth and round a small stone, perhaps for hundreds of years, for David's homemade sling. The small smooth stone was the perfect missile David would use to send to the bare forehead of the nine-foot tall giant and cause his demise. The giant's gods (his spear, shield, sword, helmet, and brass body coverings) along with his training and long experience failed him when confronted by a youngster with no military training and no combat equipment. None of this was an accident.

David's strength and power were internal. He trusted God to deliver him with a simple sling and a small stone. This battle, ending with a small stone, led to victory for the army of Israel and total defeat and humiliation for the Philistines. Following this, David would become the King's armor bearer and eventually the King of Israel. God was faithful toward David and his nation of Israel.

And so He is toward each of us who trust in Him and recognize His faithfulness.

God is truly faithful to His Word and its preservation. His faithfulness to His word, written and in the hearts of His people, is displayed with individuals, groups, and nations. In this context, the story of the small city of Libna, around the period of 710 B. C., illustrates this. The story is found in Isiah 36-37.

Libna was a walled city of refuge for the persecuted spiritual remnant of Israel. All spiritual scripts and related materials of Israel had been taken there for protection. There were no soldiers and no military armaments. Assyria withdrew from a military attack on Jerusalem and turned the battle toward Libna with a war machine of 185,000 soldiers with powerful armaments. The inhabitants of Libna were powerless against the Assyrians. The Assyrian army prepared to overrun the walls and to attack the next morning. That night, through the faithfulness of God, the Angel of the Lord quietly slew the entire Assyrian army. The next morning, the field around Libna were littered with bodies, and tens of thousands of weapons of war.

Why would God do such a thing? It was God's word within a poor man's soul that prompted the actions the Lord took over 270 years later during the siege of Libna. The poor man remains unknown to the world and unappreciated for his deliverance of Libna. But in the faithfulness of God, He did not forget the "poor wise man." The poor wise man possessed a soul filled with God's word. God remembered the content of his soul. God honored him over two centuries later with this victory.

In the Libna event, the nation Israel prospered almost unbelievably by God providing the spoils of the destroyed enemy, Assyria, to go to Israel. In the fields around Libna, there were left tens of thousands of chariots, horses, battle helmets, swords, shields, armor, bows and arrows, spears, and much other warfare equipment. Thousands of pieces of warrior's clothing remained for future use. All this went to Israel to form the most powerful military in the world at the time. This was the faithfulness of God toward His people of Israel. This was the result of the words of God in the soul of the "poor wise man" of Ecclesiastes over 270 years before. God does not forget. His memory is forever.

The people of Libna were delivered along with their sacred documents concerning the words of God. In all this, God was and is faithful to preserve His word. He did this for each of us.

"The words of the Lord are pure words: as silver tried in a furnace of earth, purified seven times. Thou shalt keep them O Lord, thou shalt preserve them from this generation forever." Psalm 12:6-7

"The grass withereth, the flower fadeth, but the word of our God shall stand forever." Isaiah 40:8

"Heaven and earth may pass away, but my words shall not pass away." Matthew 24:35

Why is it so difficult to forgive someone who has hurt us? In Mark 11:25 and Luke 6:37, God says that if we don't forgive others for their wrongdoings towards us, then as a result, God will not be faithful in forgiving us of our wrongdoings. With this divine proclamation, it would seem to us that forgiveness is a "must do" in the Christian lifestyle. However, it still remains a difficult "task" to do. We try to be faithful to God's Word, but as humans, we find it hard to do because we have been hurt badly.

We have been hurt and/or embarrassed and our inner selves have been devastated. Some of us seek revenge—to get even with the person. All we seem to think about is our "sad hurt" or the means of getting even. Day in and day out—our minds seem to be obsessed with the idea.

★★★★★★★ ★★★★★★★★ ★★★★★★★★★ ★★★★★★★★

Faith is trusting God
even when we don't
understand His plan.
-----anonymous

★★★★★★★ ★★★★★★★★★ ★★★★★★★★★ ★★★★★★★★

And yet, one of God's essence is His faithfulness in forgiving us. If we are to be more like Christ, then forgiveness is a divine "must"—wholeheartedly. God's faithfulness in forgiving us allows us to have a pure, clean, and wholesome life connected to God.

While we may, at times, have difficulty in forgiving a specific individual, we have to remember that God has done it for us many times over. God is faithful to honor us when we are faithful in forgiving others when we have been wronged or misunderstood.

The greatest act of true forgiveness in the Bible is Luke 23:34. After Jesus had been beaten and nailed to the cross, He asked God the Father to forgive the soldiers for they know not what they were truthfully doing. The immense love of Christ is demonstrated on that horrific day. My mind cannot even come close to understanding the depth of such love and of forgiveness that Christ had for His tormentors. On behalf of the request from Christ, the result of forgiveness would certainly be granted. God is faithful.

Such an act of forgiveness must be part of our spiritual DNA if we are to grow and mature spiritually. Being able to forgive others of any wrongdoings frees us up to being more and more like the character of God. God is faithful to ensure such a promotion in life.

CHAPTER 16

Thoughts From Others

I grew up in a very disjointed family, but I did not realize it because it was all I knew. My childhood was a mixture of good and bad. I have never doubted the love my mother had for me and my sisters. I have never taken for granted the blessings from my siblings and of our love and protection for one another.

I was born into a single-parent family with three older sisters. My mother, having been widowed just two months prior to my birth, was overwhelmed by the sudden death of my father and of the responsibility of four young children. During my childhood, I began to question who my "real" father was. I learned of his death from my mom.

In 1986, mom was diagnosed with lung cancer and died that spring. This was traumatic for me. I felt her loss deeply. I was 26 years old at the time of my mother's death. Life continued as my siblings and I parented each other through life's obstacles and joys. Friendships grew, family strengthened, and life blossomed.

As I approached my 40th birthday, I decided I would like to see where my father was buried. I started my search to locate the cemetery. I found out it was in Alabama. After several online searches and phone calls, I heard a response from a Mr. Gilbert on the other end of the phone. When I announced *"I am the youngest child of Edward Maurice Burke. Do you know if he is buried in your cemetery?"* He replied quickly, *"Well, yeah! All the Burkes are buried here."* He suggested that I call my cousin, D. T. Richey, to ask about any family members still alive. He provided my cousin's phone number to me without hesitation. I sat stunned after hanging up from that call.

I prayed for God to lead me—to give me wisdom and guidance in what I should do—call or ignore the line that was thrown to me? I felt that I was to call—I had to call! With trembling hands and a resolve in my heart, I dialed the number. An elderly gentleman answered. I announced who I was. Before I could say another word, this gentle voice replied, *"I know who you are. We've been looking for you for 40 years."* I was stunned—speechless. What I discovered over the next two hours of talking with my cousin was that I had over 70 cousins still living. My cousin informed me that they all meet each year for a family reunion in Alabama.

Eighteen years have passed since that conversation with my cousin. I have missed only three reunions. So, without my search, D.T. and I would never have met, and the family would not ever have known what became of us. We also would never have known any of them.

God orchestrated each piece of this journey—every thread of my life has been woven through God's design, and I am convinced of it to my very being. This has been an amazing journey, and I am overwhelmed with God's loving kindness, mercy, and grace.

--Julie Burke Farber

★★★★★ ★★★★★ ★★★★★ ★★★★★

At one time in my life, I was in a very unhappy marriage. I had tried several times to take my two daughters and leave. The relationship affected me mentally, and I reached a point where I wanted to end my life. I took a handful of sleeping pills and went to a movie theater, sitting there waiting for the movie to end so I could go get a drink, sit down, and take the pills. There in the same theater was none other than my brother, Bob. I thought, "What on earth was he doing here in the middle of the day?" "Oh good, he didn't see me. He's walking the other way. Oh no! he's turned around and now he sees me."

"What are you doing here?" he asked.

I showed him the pills and told him what I was planning to do.

He said, *"Come on home with me. We need to talk."*

What were the odds of my brother being at the theater at that exact time?

Shortly after that, I made my escape from Florida to Virginia with my two daughters. Good things have a way of coming out of bad things. I have had the honor of counseling women who were going through domestic violence in their homes. They would come to a local Abuse Shelter, where I worked, for help. I worked with them as long as it took them to get back on their feet. God works in mysterious ways.

---Betty Noble Card

*****   *****   ******   *******

Daddy's Girl

My father had always been a seemingly strong healthy guy who loved life to its fullest and was a blast to be around. He'd always been there for me in every twist and turn of life, regardless of the circumstances. He was even my golfing, boating, hiking, Bible study, and travel buddy. My dad was always the life of the party, loved by all.

A few months before the Lord called him hone, his energy and memory started to drastically fail him. I spent every Saturday helping my parents in any way I could. Dad was hospitalized for his last several weeks, and no matter how exhausted I was, after a long work day, I would usually go spend a couple hours in the evening, watching him fade away before my eyes. On the morning of November 6, 2015, I was called to the front office of the school where I was teaching. As soon as I saw my husband, Mike, standing there to greet me with a solemn look on his face, I knew the Lord had just called my sweet daddy home, I knew that my dad's suffering was over. My heart was suddenly floating in a giant puddle of tears on the floor.

When Mike and I arrived at the nursing facility where my father had been, my brother Steve was there with the body, patiently awaiting our arrival. After having been there for a while, it was time that we left. As we walked outside of the nursing facility, numb and completely broken on the inside, I clearly heard God's still small voice say, "*Kathy, look up!*"

As I looked up into the bright blue sky, I saw fluffy white clouds in the perfect shape of an angel. I knew they were clouds, but were those clouds really just coincidental? God talks about there being angels here among us in many different passages of His Word. I couldn't help wonder if that was the angel who had just taken my daddy home. To me, it was clear that God had allowed this to be a sweet assurance that dad was now safely home in the arms of the Lord and that the spiritual legacy that my father had begun was now ours to carry on.

As the bag pipes played on that chilly fall afternoon at Florida National Cemetery, we were all very broken, yet had a peace that passes all human understanding. My brother had his arm around my mom, as she was handed the flag presented to her in memory of her brave Marine husband who courageously served our country during the Korean War. As difficult as all that was, we were reminded of God's goodness, faithfulness, and the legacy set before us.

Kathy Dillon Lischer

****** ******* ******** ********

It was on a Sunday evening during the church service that I remember going forward and telling the pastor that I wanted to accept Jesus into my heart. I remember a pull on my heart that I had never felt before.

As I went into high school, the church hired a new youth pastor. I became more involved in the youth group over the next couple of years. I became extremely close to not only other youth in the group, but also with many of the youth group adult leaders. While we had many great times of fun and fellowship, it was always a major part of our youth group to learn Biblical principles.

It wasn't until my senior year in high school when I was elected as the president of our youth group that would be the defining time in my Christian life that would prepare me for life in more ways than I ever thought of during those early years.

During my senior year as president of the youth group, the youth pastor would pour into me personally one-on-one attention of life lessons and leadership in more ways that I would not truly realize until later in my adult life.

I went on in life over the next 20 to 30 years of my life to have a rewarding career in law enforcement. I had many times with those in which God would use what

I was taught in those early youth group years to impact to others.

My life really did not hit me so much until I was nearing 50 years old and had been diagnosed with a rare cancer. It was during the next few years as I battled that cancer that many times of feeling that I could not go on any longer. I began to truly see how God used my early years under the youth pastor's care, and his willingness to teach me, plus build me up as a young man that truly carried me through my battle.

Not only the youth pastor but three other key men that I had looked up to had taught me more than I had ever realized: Cecil Yates, Mark Sink, and George Owens. They were all in law enforcement.

I am now retired from law enforcement with over 30 years in the career field. I believe God used my time of battling cancer that He had NEVER left me or forsook me. God had had been there all along, working and teaching me through the four men. I have also come to know particularly over the past three years how God used me in the very same way He used the four men in my life to impact the lives of many others. I can see now how God, as a result of my being faithful and learning what He was teaching me through others, to in turn pour into others life lessons, while pointing them toward Jesus Christ. It has become so evident in my life how God has placed many people in my life over the years to be a very important part of my life.

As I look back over my life, I can remember having had many ups and downs but that all along God has been right there by my side, never once leaving me. God also placed a very special lady in my life. As a young, married couple, we took Joshua 24:15 as our marriage life passage--**...as for me and my house, we will serve the Lord.**

As we go through life, we need to see who God puts around us to use in our life. We need to always remember them and to be thankful for them. In addition, we need to allow God to use us in others' lives that He places on our paths.

---Jeff Hosfeld

******* ******* ******* ******

Over two years ago, God led me to meet Angie—a friend of a lifetime. We are similar in many ways—one is that we both like to talk—non-stop. God has always placed teachers into my life, and Angie has become one. I knew that I had hit the jackpot in a divine friendship not long after we met. God opened the door of a wonderful relationship.

Angie has the most amazing personality. To say that she is kind and caring is an understatement. As we got to know one another, Angie blessed my life with unconditional love. She is non-judgmental which allows me to express my genuine emotions and thoughts. God is indeed alive—He has provided me a confidant.

I am in the process of becoming a better writer, and Angie is very patient and understanding during the process of helping me. Our friendship is not only based on mutual respect but also on our spiritual relationship.

God is indeed Alive!
----Michelle Santana

★★★★★ ★★★★★★ ★★★★★★ ★★★★★★★

CHAPTER 17

Wisdom

Wisdom is a faculty of the mind that takes known information and puts it to the very best use for the most admirable ends. The quality of each decision is dependent upon the quality and type of information upon which each decision is made and implemented. Godly wisdom is extremely reliable since God **only** thinks in absolute truth. His thinking is complete, perfect, and without error. It provides for divine direction, peace, happiness, and civility within the lives of nations, groups, and individuals. Godly wisdom is available to those who follow and trust Him. He had provided guidelines of information and wisdom to be written in a Book and made available to those who desire to know Him, of how He thinks, and of how He operates over time.

The believer is instructed to get Godly wisdom. There are listed benefits for doing so: divine understanding, promotions, honor, and ornaments of grace—Proverbs 4:7-9. Godly wisdom is the right use and exercise of knowledge coming forth from the mind of God to accomplish His own objectives and His plan for mankind. God's wisdom includes the faculty of discerning and of judging what is consistent with His righteousness and what is proper and useful to His grace plan and operations. Wisdom is "reason made perfect by knowledge." It is the knowledge and use of what is best, just, proper, and conducive to human prosperity and happiness. This is contrasted with the wisdom of this world which is mere human learning regarding worldly matters and information. This is called "fleshly wisdom."

The wisdom of this world is separately distinguished from the wisdom of God. It involves the carnal policies of men, their crafts, and artifices promoting temporal interests. "Fleshly wisdom" is guided by "the ways of the world." This predetermines functions and operations in the world apart from Godliness. Ultimately, man's efforts apart from God bring about disappointment, chaos, violence, and death. Apart from the evil man (Genesis 3:17-19), there is "another wisdom" pictured in Proverbs which is described as the "strange woman." She works subtly to draw individuals away from and replace the wisdom of God—Proverbs 2:16-19, 7:9-23.

Our Father in Heaven truly desires to share with us His absolute knowledge and wisdom. He has provided much of His knowledge in the Bible. Through His Word, He admonishes the believer to read and to study in order to discover what is His thinking and how to use Godly information in life. The more one studies and learns, the greater grows our own Godly wisdom.

In Proverbs 1:7, one learns how God feels about those who seek to know and to understand His Word and about those individuals who do not—**"The fear of the Lord is the beginning of knowledge: but fools despise (Godly) wisdom and instruction."** When studying God's Word, our knowledge of Him and what He is doing is expanding. Along with this expansion, our Godly wisdom is also growing. Many areas of our spiritual life begin to change. We begin a spiritual transformation in how we think and how we live (Romans 12:1-2). It is what our Father desires in each of us and actually expects. We begin to have a vastly different outlook and perspective on our environment and the individuals who cross our path each day. This is the impact Godly wisdom begins to make within each of us. We begin to think as our Father thinks. The greater our knowledge, the greater our fitness may be used by our Father.

As one grows in Godly information, he or she also expands one's Godly understanding. The individual gains wisdom's clarity through the virtues of discretion and discernment (Proverbs 2:1-11). With Godly discretion, one is able to pick and to choose between matters that measure up to God's righteous standards and discard those that do not. This enables each person to critically judge what is correct and proper, always using caution in particular with regards to one's own conduct. This is Godly wisdom in action through the life of a person who seeks to gain in His wisdom.

In becoming a discerning person, the individual sees and understands the differences between good and evil, truth and falsehood. Godly discernment looks through appearances and sees character, deeds, actions, and their differences and their true motives. The person who has both Godly discretion and Godly discernment is not easily misled because he or she is not imposed upon by appearances. This is divine clarity as a part of the wisdom of God.

As one grows in grace, knowledge, and wisdom of God, he or she finds true human happiness. This happiness we find in the wisdom of God. With this happiness comes spiritual riches and honor.

There are five areas of basic spiritual labor opportunities in which we should become involved. Each of these five proceeds from the wisdom God shares with us to provide for our living the spiritual life as it should be lived. These become five spiritual virtues of Godly wisdom that form and shape our Christian life and character.

The first virtue of Godly wisdom is that of **selflessness**. Instead of promoting personal desires above the interests of others, selflessness places the interests and values of others above one's own life. Other persons come first. Such actions of wisdom are noted by everyone. It cannot be missed. It speaks to one's personal values, character, integrity, promises, and vows and reflects respect, value, and honor toward other persons. It illustrates the love and wisdom of God in action through a believe in Jesus Christ. The Apostle Paul states: ***"For I say, through the grace given unto me to every man that is among you, not to think of himself more highly than he ought to think; but***

to think soberly, according as God hath dealt to every man the measure of faith" (Romans 12:3).

The second virtue of Godly wisdom is that of **lovingkindness**. This is the virtue that possesses an instant sense of warmness, generosity, affection, benevolence, and amiability. The element of lovingkindness is an invitation to befriend a person and to establish a reassured relationship.

Lovingkindness reflects Godly care and concern toward another. This is how one "honours" another person, placing the other person's interests above that of one's own. This reflects the wisdom of God in dealing with the human race. Consider the work of Christ on the cross. He put all the needs of humanity above His personal needs. His greatest interest and concern were that of others. This was "the grand expression" of lovingkindness.

The third virtue of Godly wisdom is that of **tenderheartedness**. This virtue has a deep interest in the welfare and advancement of another person. It is an affection from wisdom that comes forth with a warm heart for others.

Tenderheartedness goes well beyond the physical aspects of the other person. It goes to the spiritual well-being of another individual: his knowledge of the plan of God for his life; his relationship with our Father in heaven; and his interest in the advancement of his spiritual edification and understanding of God's Word.

Intercessory prayer can play a big role in this area of Godly wisdom.

The fourth virtue of wisdom is that of **meekness**. Meekness is a reflection of great inner character, integrity, and personal inner strength. This individual seeks to assist and to elevate the other person to a much higher level of civil thought and action rather than seeking revenge from a wrongdoing. On the cross, Jesus prayed for his accusers saying, ***Forgive them Father, for they know not what they do.***" Such is the gold standard for expressing meekness as we go through trials in life.

One who lives a life of meekness is not a coward, is not intimidated, and is not anxious to seek revenge once injured. One's thinking should be in the other person's best interests. This is the wisdom of our Father. His heart is our heart. His wisdom is our wisdom.

The fifth virtue of Godly wisdom is that of **benevolent goodness**. This virtue overcomes the powerful lust pattern to take something of great value away from another. The wisdom virtue of benevolent goodness surpasses and overpowers the greed involved in such a matter. As one studies and learns of these wisdom virtues, that person's life is changed forever. Romans 12:2—***"And be not conformed to the world: but be ye transformed by the renewing of your mind, that ye may prove what is that good, and acceptable, and perfect will of God."***

****** ******* ******* ********

It's the unexpected kindness
from the unexpected person
at the unexpected moment
that makes someone feel special

---Anonymous

CHAPTER 18

Heirship of God

As believers in Jesus Christ, our Father in heaven has provided us with many benefits for our spiritual understanding, discernment, and direction. Not only has He made great promises for special benefits to us for this purpose, but He is also working to bring each of us to "fitness" for His use in our future lives in Heaven. These promises and benefits are numerous. This is for our godly living as his sons and daughters. As such, this is "our heirship of God" which is found in Romans 8:14-17.

Regarding godly heirship, we need to remember Jesus' words to his twelve Apostles at the last supper in the upper room just prior to His crucifixion. Concerning the drink, He stated *"This cup is the new testament in my blood."* Jesus was aware that the time of His suffering and death was at hand, including His death, burial, and resurrection. He knew the purpose in what He would endure was necessary to provide **redemption** for the human race. His comments to the Apostles at that moment were appropriate for the suppertime occasion in the upper room.

A testament is similar to a will. It concerns a solemn, authentic instrument, normally in writing, in which a person declares his "will" as to the disposal of his estate and affects after his death. There are always beneficiaries which inherit the estate. To be valid, the testament must be made when the testator is of sound mind. It must be "subscribed, witnessed, and published" in such manner as law prescribes. At the supper table with His Apostles, Jesus was taking care of these details of validation.

The Bible reminds us that we are "heirs" of God: heirs of the promise, heirs of righteousness, heirs of salvation, and joint heirs with Christ. Eternal life is a part of our heirship—Titus 3:7. All areas of our heirship are the result of the cross work of Jesus Christ. We have available many heirship benefits, such as being ransomed, justified, sanctified, and reconciled. We are designated a particular people. The power of sin in our lives has been broken. We possess a special sonship ministry. In addition, we are declared servants of righteousness with being ambassadors of Christ. We have inherited a complete written word of God. We are under grace, **not** under the law. Additionally, we will share joint heirship with Christ in Heaven.

These were some of the many matters Jesus had on his mind as He sat and talked to His Apostles at the supper table in the upper room. It was a matter which He must face, endure, and be successful in order to provide for the completion of the plan of His Father concerning the human race. It was also an issue in which He was trying to get His Apostles to be aware, to comprehend, and to appreciate as it occurred.

It refreshes the spirit and soul when one considers the preparations our Father has made for our future roles in Heaven as a part of the Church, the body of Christ. We will be existing in our new resurrection bodies. Heaven and earth will be brought to function together in perfect harmony to the glory of God in the "dispensation of the fullness of times." These two diverse realms will be gathered together and unified for the purpose of functioning together for God's glory. The earth and Heaven will function together in joint activities in accordance with their original design.

There is more of our inheritance from our Father in Heaven. It is endless and forever. His "kindness toward us through Christ Jesus" will have further manifestations in the ages to come and the "dispensation of the fullness of times" will showcase them to "the praise and glory of His grace." Our Father's plans will bring them to pass. All of these matters are for His glory. We will be very involved in these matters as a member of the Body of Christ and as part of our Godly inheritance.

The magnificence of God and the glory of His character and essence, both in view of what He has done and what He will yet to do "in the ages to come," will be an all-absorbing, all-encompassing matter. All will be "to the glory of God."

CHAPTER 19

Merchandise of God

As an individual studies and learns God's Word, divine wisdom not only provides him or her with Godly understanding but is also the source of true happiness—Proverbs 3:13-18. Godly wisdom provides us with divine **understanding, discernment, and discretion**. These are to be used as we learn to think like God and to labor with Him in His ongoing operations in this life. We are to "cry out" after knowledge and "lift up our voices" for understanding—Proverbs 2:3.

God is the source of **Godly worth**. He is also the perfect **Godly image** and the source of **Godly esteem**. His divine power resides in these personal properties. It is His desire to share these personal divine properties with us as believers in Jesus Christ. These properties are available to each of us should we have the earnest desire to seek them. God's desire is to reproduce these characteristics in the life of each of us and for us to use and to illustrate in our lives towards others. We refer to them as **"merchandise of God"**—Proverbs 3:14.

With divine understanding, we correctly view life from our Father's thinking and perspective. With divine discernment, we are able to choose between right and wrong, good and bad, divine and corrupt. With divine discretion, we are able to critically judge all things as to being proper, of being divine in nature or sinfully corrupt, to be able to sense evil threats and avoid corruption, to choose the correct divine paths to follow, and to evaluate life's circumstances that each of us face each day. This is "power for living."

As a believer in Jesus Christ, these matters of **divine worth, divine image,** and **divine esteem** are available to us as we grow in grace and knowledge of the truth of God and realize what He has provided for us. In Genesis 2:26-28, God made man in His own **image** and His own likeness. Man was to "have dominion over every living thing." Furthermore, he was to be ruler of earth. Given great authority, man was to live a Godly life, to "think like God, live like God, and labor with God." There was great purpose of God for man to so exist at that moment in time.

Unfortunately, man rebelled. Because of man's rebellion, God instituted a revelation program utilizing individual believers to make known and to accomplish His will on earth. In doing so, He made it clear that He was **"The God**, the most high God, possessor of heaven and earth"—Genesis 14:18-22. He has placed it in writing for our benefit. He has made it possible for man, in an imperfect environment, to again be of **worth** to God, to live as the **image** of God, and to possess Godly **esteem.**

God exists as truth. He is "wisdom, justice, and judgment." He is the source of life and consciousness.

Having been created in His **image** and likeness, we are called upon to be like Him in practice in our lives.

In representing God, His Word teaches "renewing" the mind in selflessness, lovingkindness, tenderheartedness, meekness, and benevolent goodness. This is Godly love and charity in action which makes an impact toward others in this life. We are, or can be, of great **worth** to God. Our Godly **image** has huge impact as we continue to be of **esteem** to our Father.

While it may seem the entire world has gone mad, it is an opportune time for believers in Christ to be of great **worth** to God. He has designated us as "ambassadors of Christ" to represent Him in the world. An ambassador does not belong to the country where he is sent. We are citizens of God's heavenly kingdom. We are appointed ambassadors by God for Christ. As such, we do not enter these ambassadorial tasks to profit ourselves or to represent ourselves, but to serve the Lord Jesus Christ. Everything we do and say reflects upon Him. An ambassador is accepted not on his own merit but because of who he represents. We are not to take it personally when we are despised and rejected by those who disavow Christ. As such, we are of great **worth** to God as we represent the cause of Christ in this world.

God has provided in us divine investments as believers in Jesus Christ. All His investments in each of us is to enhance His own **worth**, **image**, and **esteem** within and through us as we submit ourselves to His plans for our lives. This is a matter of grace on our behalf. He has also declared us a peculiar people with the power of sin broken in our lives.

God has endowed us with a special "sonship" ministry, a heavenly citizenship, and an intimate relationship with Him and other believers. He has declared us servants of righteousness. He has given us His complete Word. We are now under grace. We have been made Ambassadors of Christ and possess joint heirship with Christ.

At the moment of our trusting Christ as Savior, our Father placed within us His own divine righteousness. This is our eternal spiritual insurance policy Even when we fail to measure up to His righteous standards in our lives, He forever maintains His very personal relationship with us as His sons and daughters. This makes our inner person of great **worth**. This reflects that we possess His own divine **worth**, live in his divine **image**, and carry His divine **esteem**. We are presently being "made fit" to live forever with our Father in heaven.

Considering God's personal interest in us, it is almost unbelievable that men do not seek after God. In grace He seeks them out through the preaching of His Word whereby He calls upon them to respond in faith. We are then called upon to shine the light of grace. This is who we are as possessors of our Father **worth, image**, and **esteem.** It is this life that God desires to see manifested in our mortal bodies.

The world is ever involved in bringing about an ungodly environment in which all men live and partakes.

We cannot escape it. Each member of the human race will inevitably be caused to live, to function, and to be influenced under the power of the world's view. As such, we find ourselves pressured to conform to this world environment.

However, as we "shine the light" upon and expose the world view, we reveal the truths of God's Word. We make known the standards of God righteousness. Furthermore, we make known the plan of God for our lives and how He expects us to live. This is our task as a member of the Body of Christ.

We can truly express Godly love in each of our lives.

Printed in the United States
By Bookmasters